Then a

by Margie Burton, Cathy French, and Tammy Jones

Here is my diary.

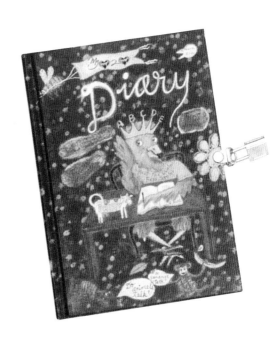

I write in it every day.

My grandma gave me her diary.
She wrote in it every day
when she was little like I am.

I like to look at what she wrote
when she was little like I am.
I like to look at her pictures, too.

My grandma wrote:
We got a new car today!
This is what it looks like:

This is what my grandma put in her diary for
January 20, 1940.

I wrote:
Here I am by our car.
I like to ride in it.

This is what I put in my diary for January 20 this year.

My grandma wrote:
I went to a baseball game.
It was so much fun!
This is what it looked like:

This is what my grandma put in her diary for April 30, 1940.

I wrote:
Today I went to a baseball game.
My team won!

This is what I put in my diary for April 30 this year.

My grandma wrote:
Here is a picture of my teacher
and my class at school.

This is what my grandma put in her diary for
June 20, 1940.

I wrote:
We did puzzles at school today.
We all had fun.

This is what I put in my diary for June 20 this year.

My grandma wrote:
We are going far away today.
We have to take a big ship
to get there.
This is what it looks like:

This is what my grandma put in her diary for
July 7, 1940.

I wrote:

We are going on a trip.
We are going far away. We have
to fly to get there.

This is what I put in my diary for July 7
this year.

My grandma wrote:
I went to the beach today.
Here is the picture I took
at the beach:

This is what my grandma put in her diary for
August 10, 1940.

I wrote:

I like to play at the beach.

I like to play in the sand.

This is what I put in my diary for August 10 this year.

My grandma wrote:
Here is a picture of our radio.
I like to listen to it.

This is what my grandma put in her diary on
October 12, 1940.

I wrote:
My mom, dad, and I watched
TV today. I like to watch TV.

This is what I put in my diary on October 12
this year.

I went to see my grandma today.
We looked at her diary and then
we looked at my diary.
It was fun to look at them.